Color Funny Doodles
Colouring Book

'Book Two: Beautiful'

Hartmut Jager

My Fat Fox Ltd
MMXV

My Fat Fox Ltd
86 Gladys Dimson House
London E7 9DF
United Kingdom
www.myfatfox.co.uk

Color Funny Doodles Colouring Book 2 Beautiful
© 2015 Hartmut Jager

http://hartmut-jager.artistwebsites.com/

The rights of Hartmut Jager to be identified as the author of this work have been asserted by him in accordance with the Copyright, Designs and Patents Act, 1988

Cover design
© 2015 Hartmut Jager

http://hartmut–jager.artistwebsites.com/

ISBN 978-1-905747-39-9

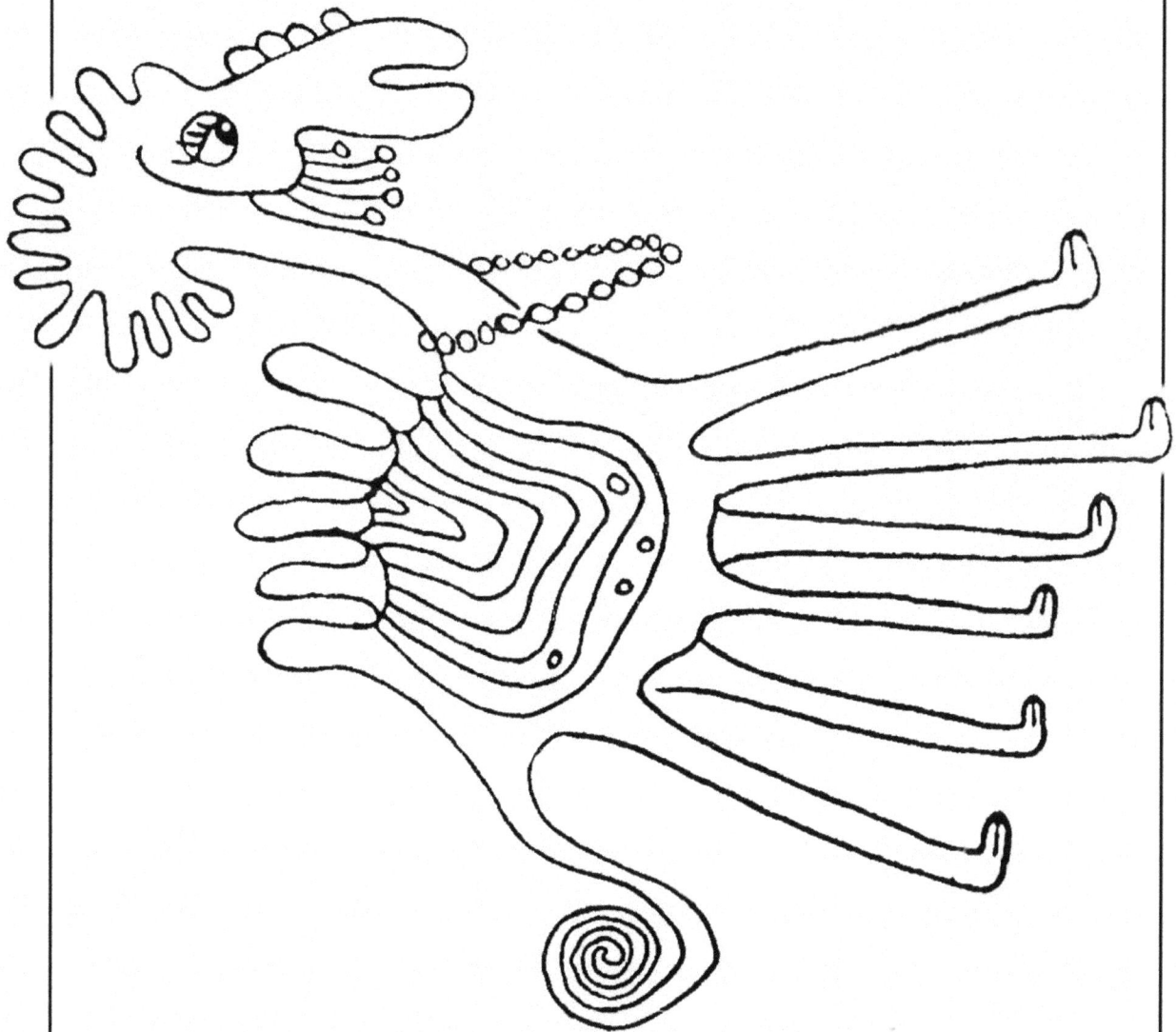

© 95 HARTMUT JÄGER

Bird conference

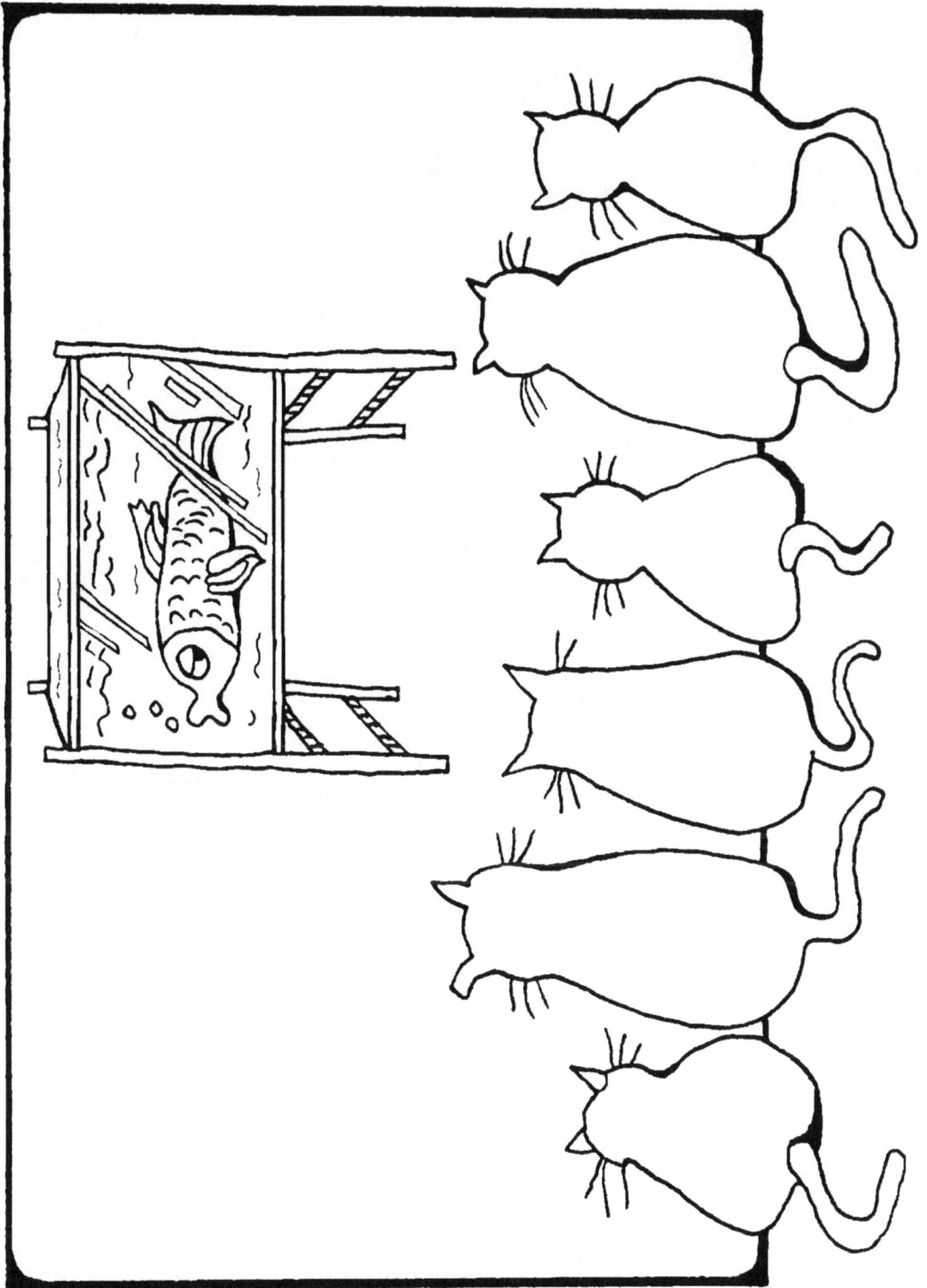

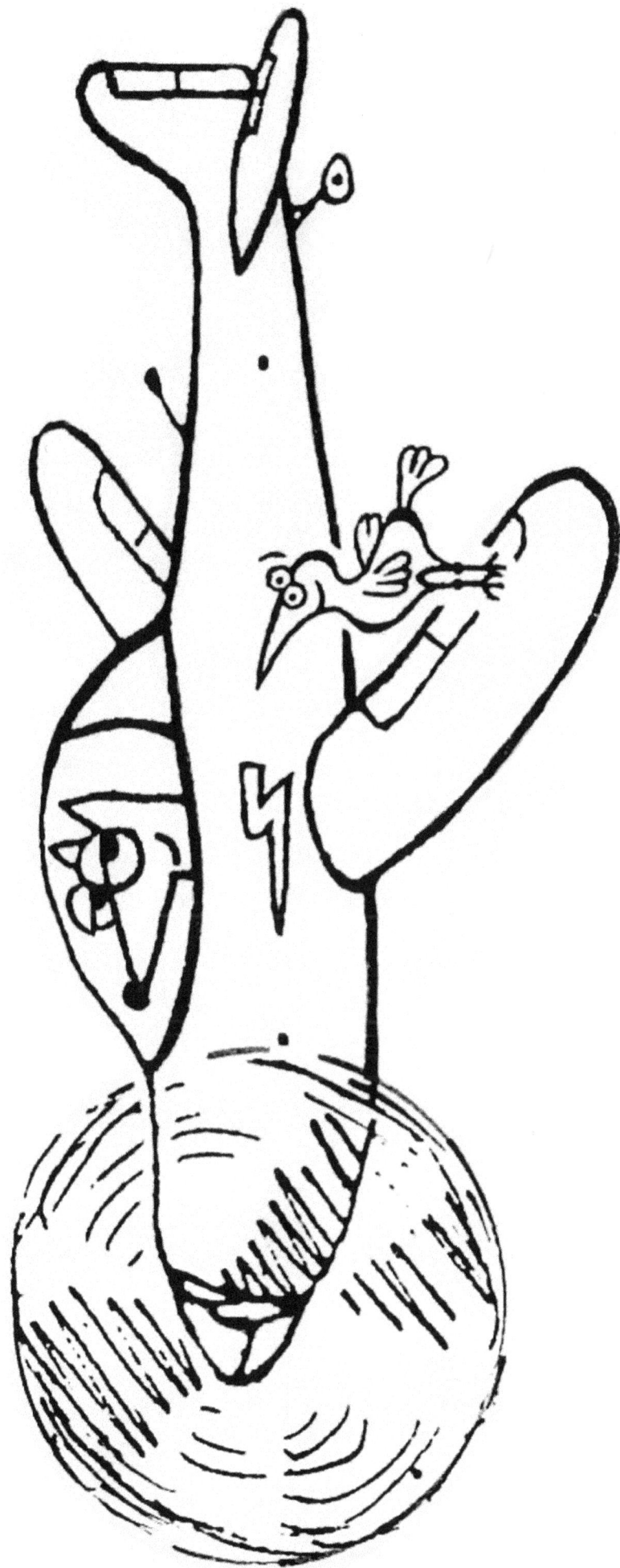

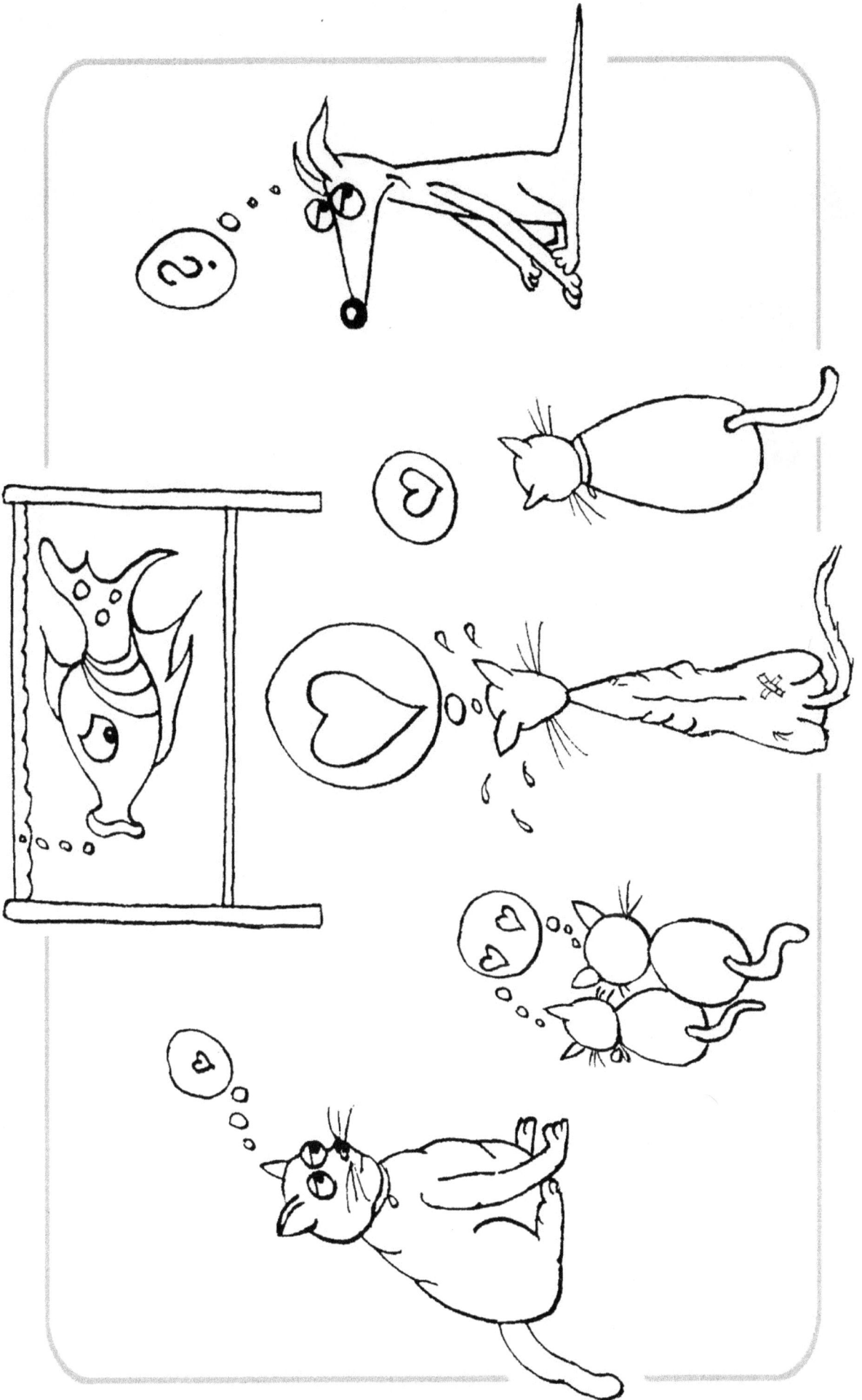

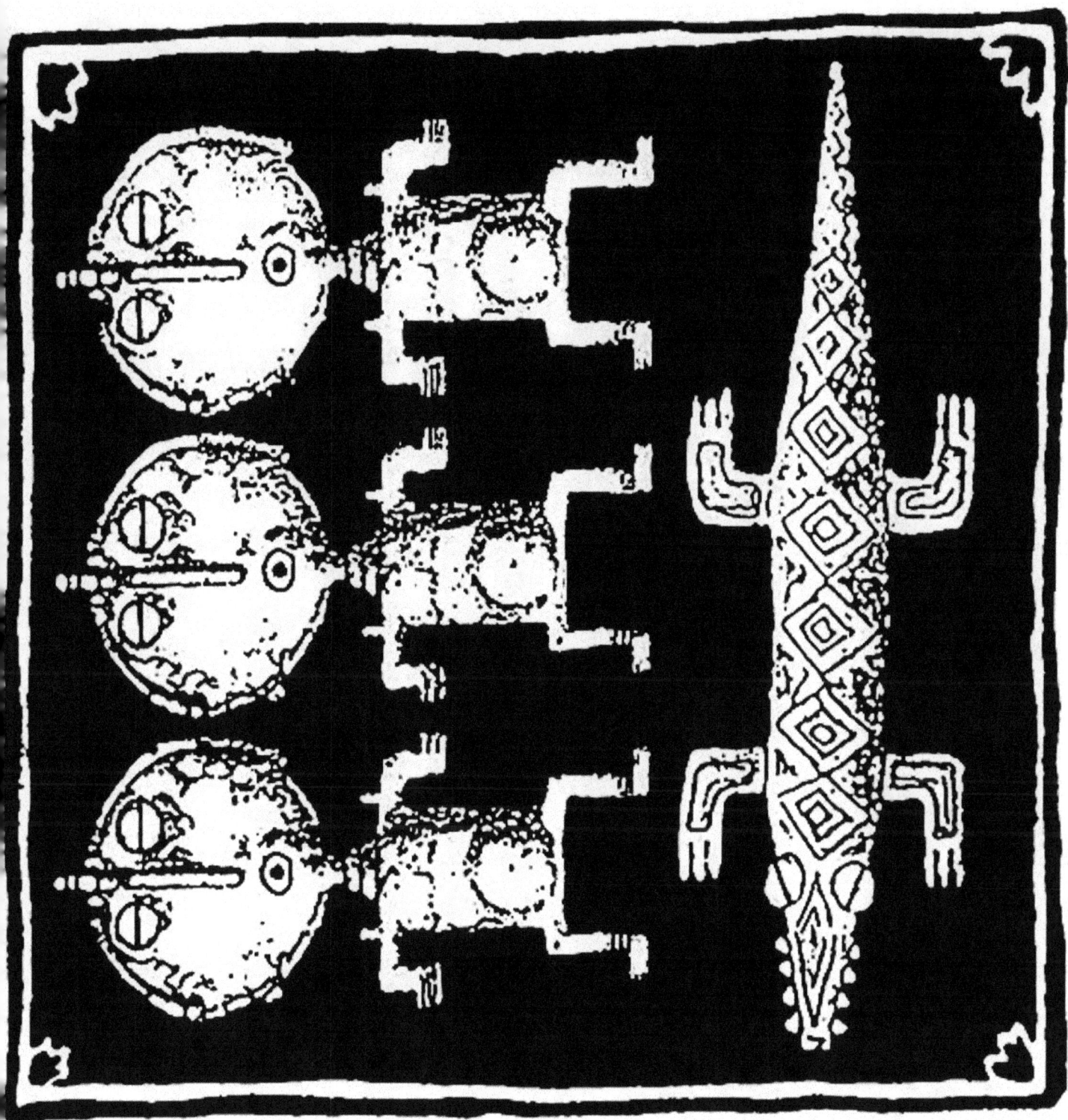

FROG DREAM

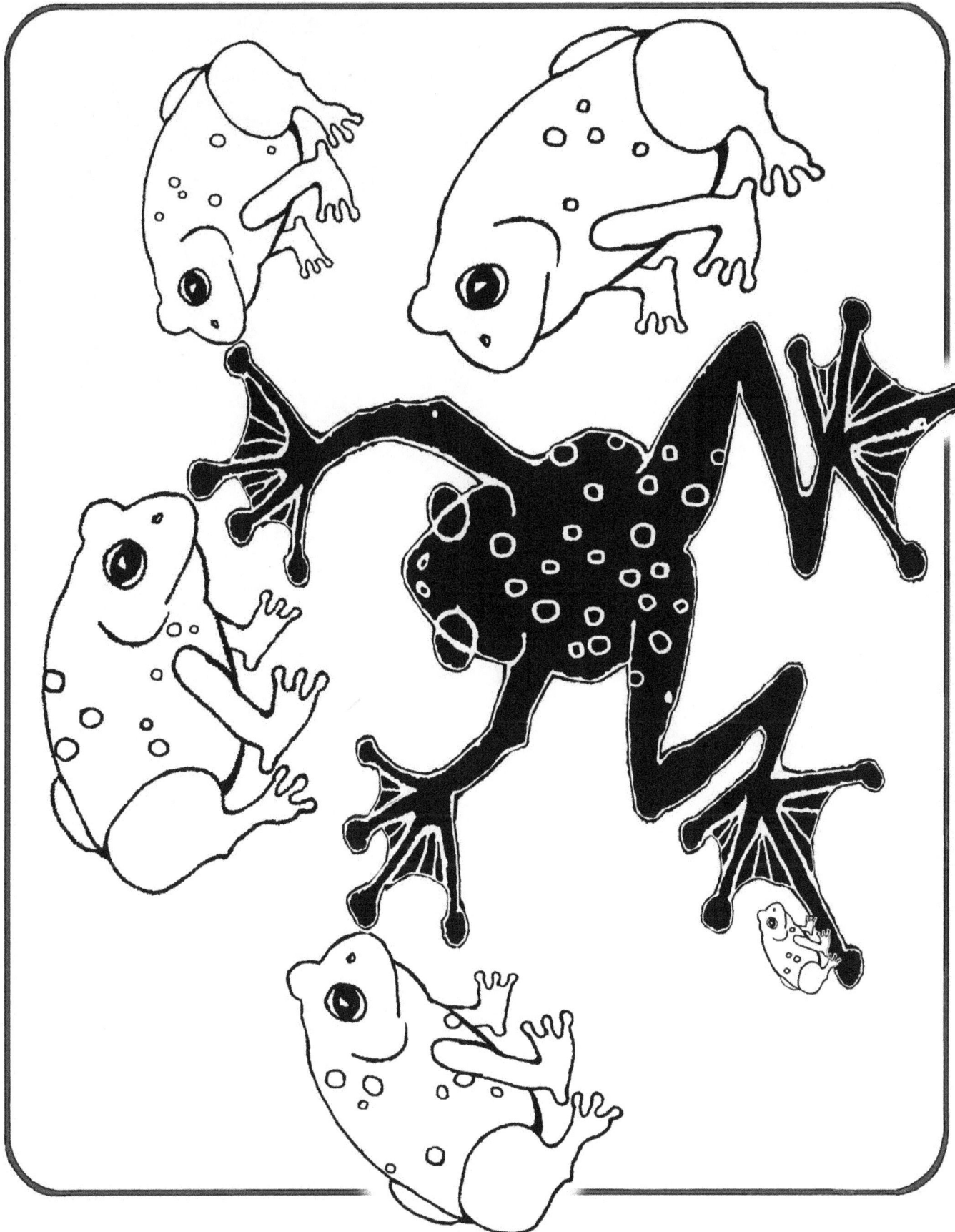

© 95 HARTMUT JAGER

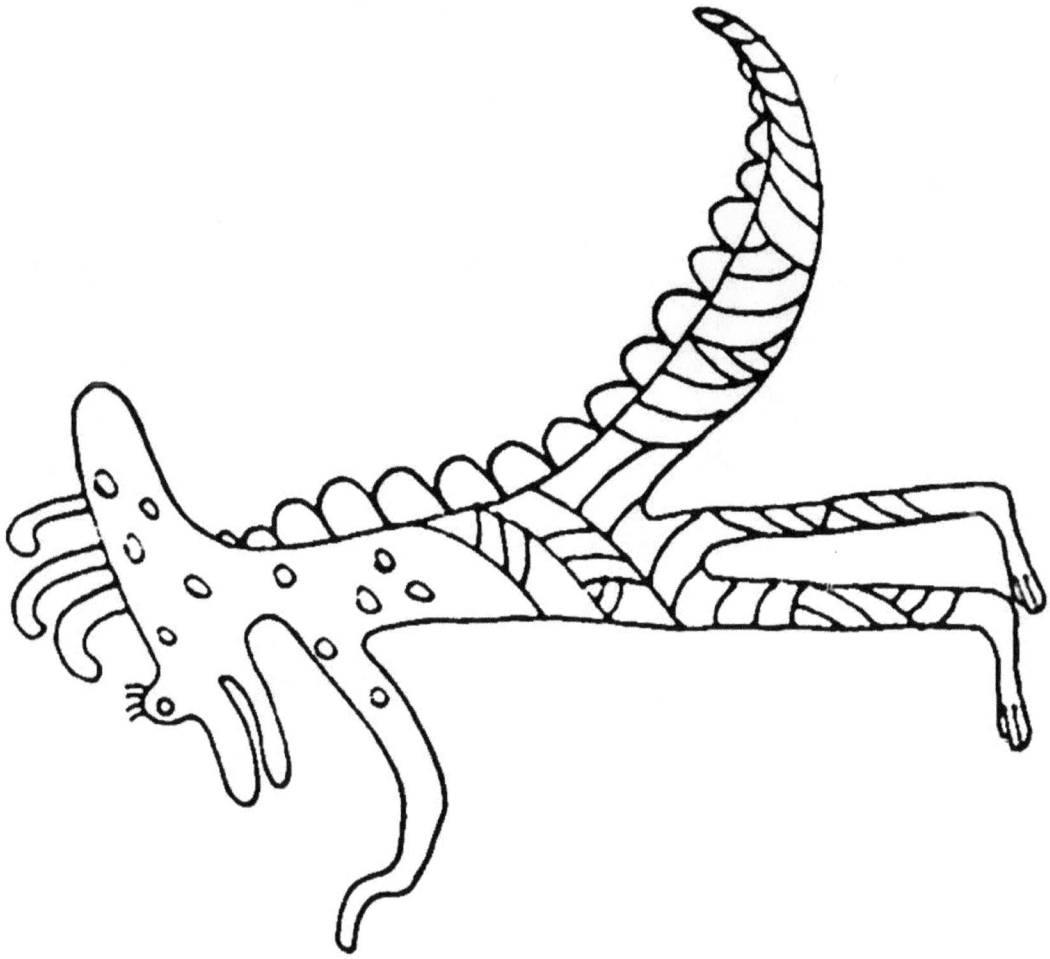

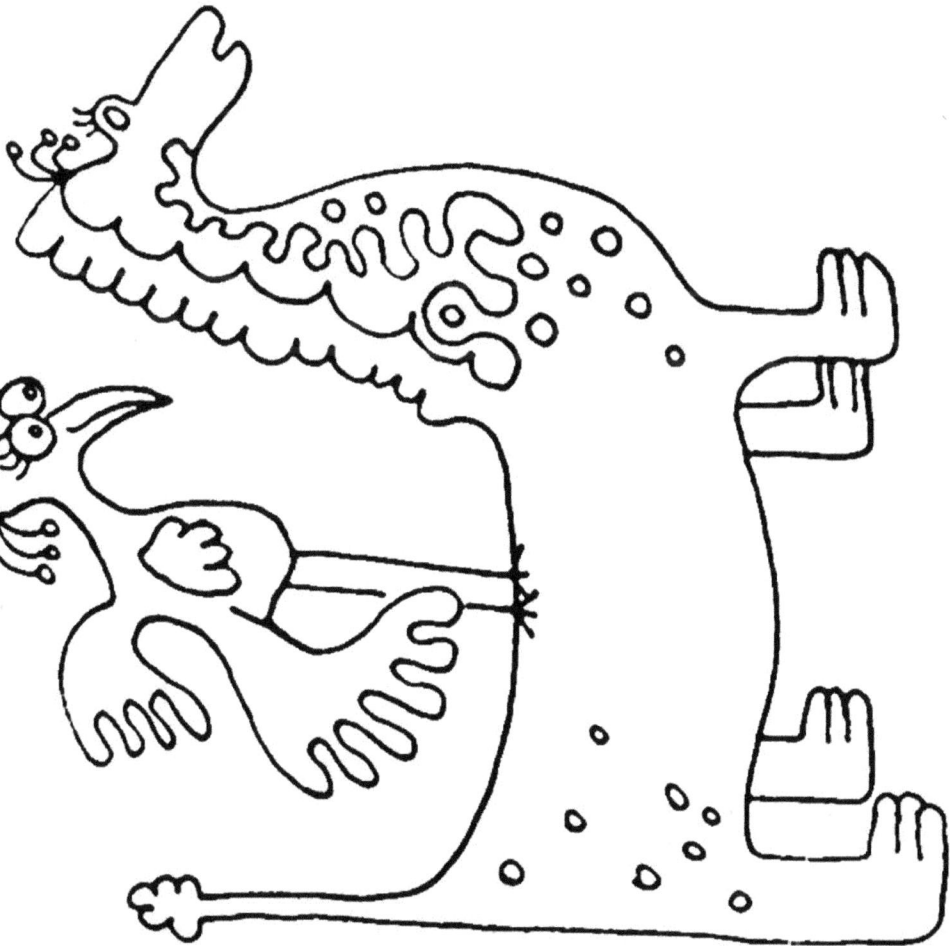

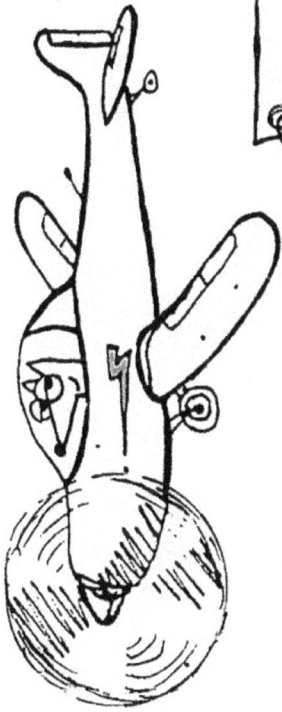

My Fat Fox
Books and Digital Media

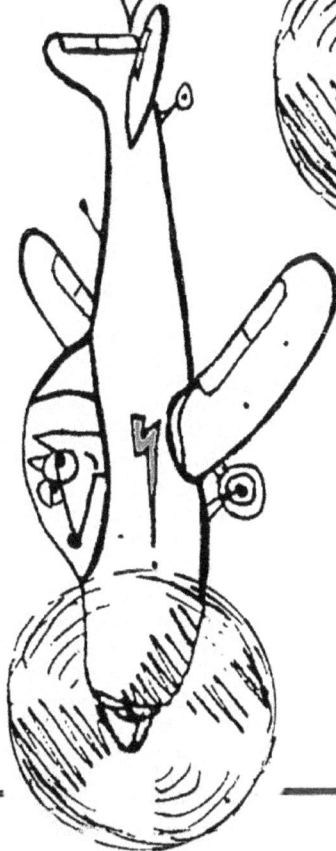

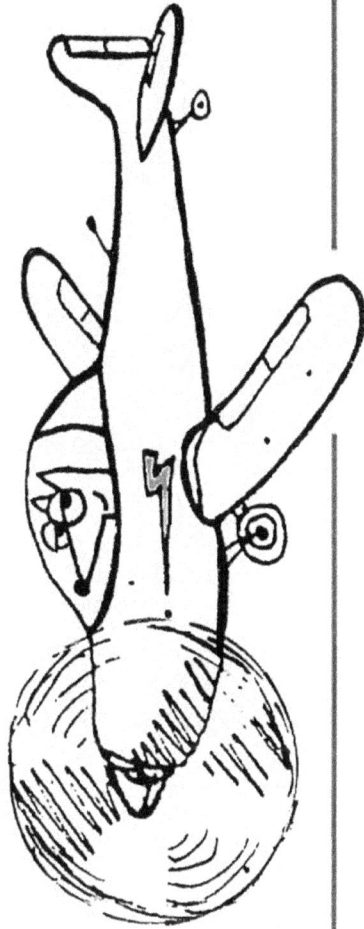